Fixing Hubble's Troubles

by Philip Stewart

Editorial Offices: Glenview, Illinois • Parsippany, New Jersey • New York, New York
Sales Offices: Needham, Massachusetts • Duluth, Georgia • Glenview, Illinois
Coppell, Texas • Sacramento, California • Mesa, Arizona

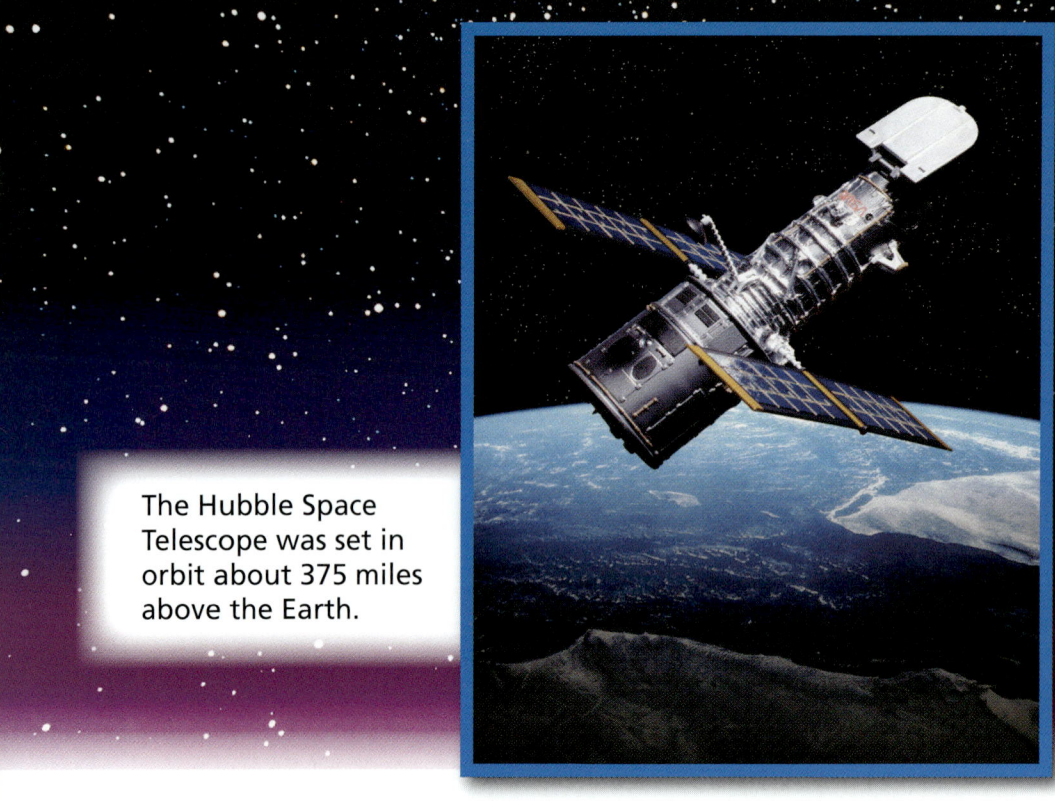

The Hubble Space Telescope was set in orbit about 375 miles above the Earth.

The Hubble Space Telescope

For hundreds of years, scientists have studied the sky with telescopes. They have learned many things, but looking out into space from the Earth has been a problem. The air—the atmosphere—changes the light that comes to the Earth and down into the telescopes. Images from distant space are not clear.

Scientists wanted clear images. They decided to put a giant telescope in space, in orbit around the Earth. This telescope would send clear images of stars and other objects in space.

---

telescopes: tools for making distant things appear closer and larger

orbit: the circular path of an object around another object

The primary mirror took three years to grind and polish.

The Space Shuttle *Discovery* carried five crew members and the Hubble Space Telescope.

The Hubble Space Telescope was made. On April 24, 1990, the Space Shuttle *Discovery* carried the telescope and released it into space.

Putting Hubble in space was a great accomplishment. Hubble was a very advanced telescope—and as large as a school bus! Its primary, or main, mirror measured almost eight feet across. Hubble also carried cameras and other instruments. These instruments would gather information and send it by radio signals to scientists on Earth.

---

instruments: tools used to do special tasks

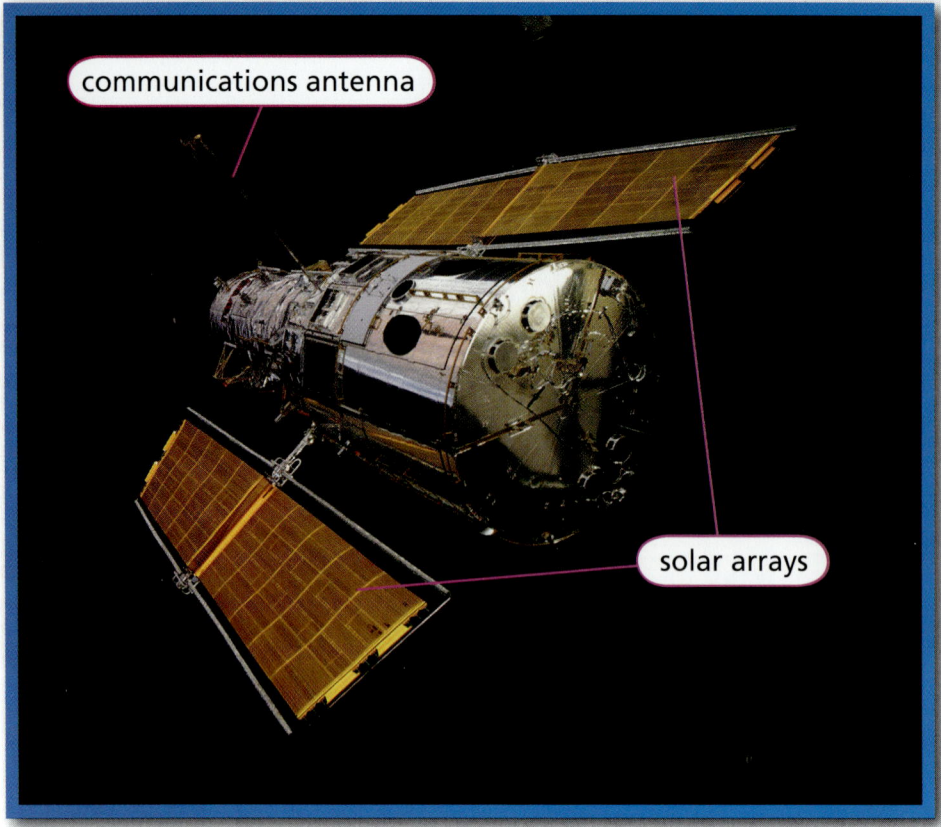

The solar arrays are the wing-like structures on either side of the telescope. A communications antenna is sticking out of the other side of Hubble.

But soon scientists discovered problems with Hubble. Hubble was not working properly. There were problems with its communications antennas, control systems, and solar arrays.

The worst problem was that Hubble was sending blurry pictures. Scientists found the problem after many tests. The primary mirror had been shaped incorrectly. It was a very small mistake, but it had a very big impact. The telescope could not send clear images.

---

blurry: not clear

Scientists knew that replacing the mirror was not possible. They decided to build new instruments. These instruments would correct Hubble's vision. They would work the same way glasses correct a person's vision. Scientists also figured out solutions for Hubble's other problems.

But repairing a telescope in space is not the same as repairing a car on a nearby street. Astronauts would have to travel into space and go to Hubble as it moved in orbit. They would have to take the new instruments and make the difficult repairs. Their journey into space would be a special mission, a trip to do important work.

Extend Language   A Multiple-Meaning Word

Missions can be places such as buildings where groups do religious or social work.

But the word *mission* can also mean "a special project that people go to do." This is the meaning in the sentence *The astronauts were sent on a mission to fix the space telescope.*

Can people besides astronauts be sent on other kinds of missions, right here on Earth?

Space Repairs

Scientists knew that astronauts would have to visit Hubble from time to time to keep it operating well. Missions to repair Hubble had been planned even before it was launched into space. That was one of the things that made Hubble so special—it was designed to be fixed in space by astronauts. It had compartments that slid out like drawers and bright yellow handrails for the astronauts to hold on to.

But no one had expected that the first mission to repair Hubble would be so complicated. Scientists carefully chose the most experienced astronauts to carry out this mission. The astronauts went up on the Space Shuttle *Endeavour* on December 2, 1993.

Astronaut Story Musgrave on the first spacewalk. He is holding on to one of Hubble's yellow handrails.

The astronauts of the first repair mission: (from left to right) Jeffrey Hoffman, Claude Nicollier, Thomas Akers, Richard Covey, Kathryn Thornton, Kenneth Bowersox, Story Musgrave.

The seven-member crew of the Space Shuttle *Endeavour* trained for more than a year before their mission. Each member had a specific role:

Richard Covey, the mission commander, would be in charge of the mission.

Ken Bowersox, the pilot, would fly the shuttle.

Claude Nicollier would move the shuttle's *robotic arm,* a special mechanical tool that carried the astronauts and equipment and grabbed objects.

Story Musgrave, the payload commander, would plan and go on *spacewalks,* or walks out in space, to fix the telescope.

Jeffrey Hoffman, Thomas Akers, and **Kathryn Thornton** would fix the telescope on spacewalks.

---

payload: things that are needed for a mission

Hubble was attached to *Endeavour*'s open payload bay so that astronauts could work on it.

After liftoff from Earth, it took two days for *Endeavour* and its crew to reach Hubble.

Endeavour came close enough to grab the space telescope. Ken Bowersox guided the shuttle to just the right distance. Claude Nicollier used the robotic arm and grabbed Hubble. He placed the telescope very carefully into the shuttle's *payload bay* for repairs. This is the huge part of the shuttle that opens to hold items in place so that astronauts can work on them.

The following day, the first team of spacewalkers, Story Musgrave and Jeffrey Hoffman, made the first repairs on Hubble. They had to replace gyroscopes on the telescope. These are the instruments that help Hubble stay steady. The two astronauts worked most of the night on this job.

The second team, Thomas Akers and Kathryn Thornton, went out the next day. They removed Hubble's solar arrays and then installed new ones.

Astronaut Kathryn Thornton works on Hubble during the second spacewalk.

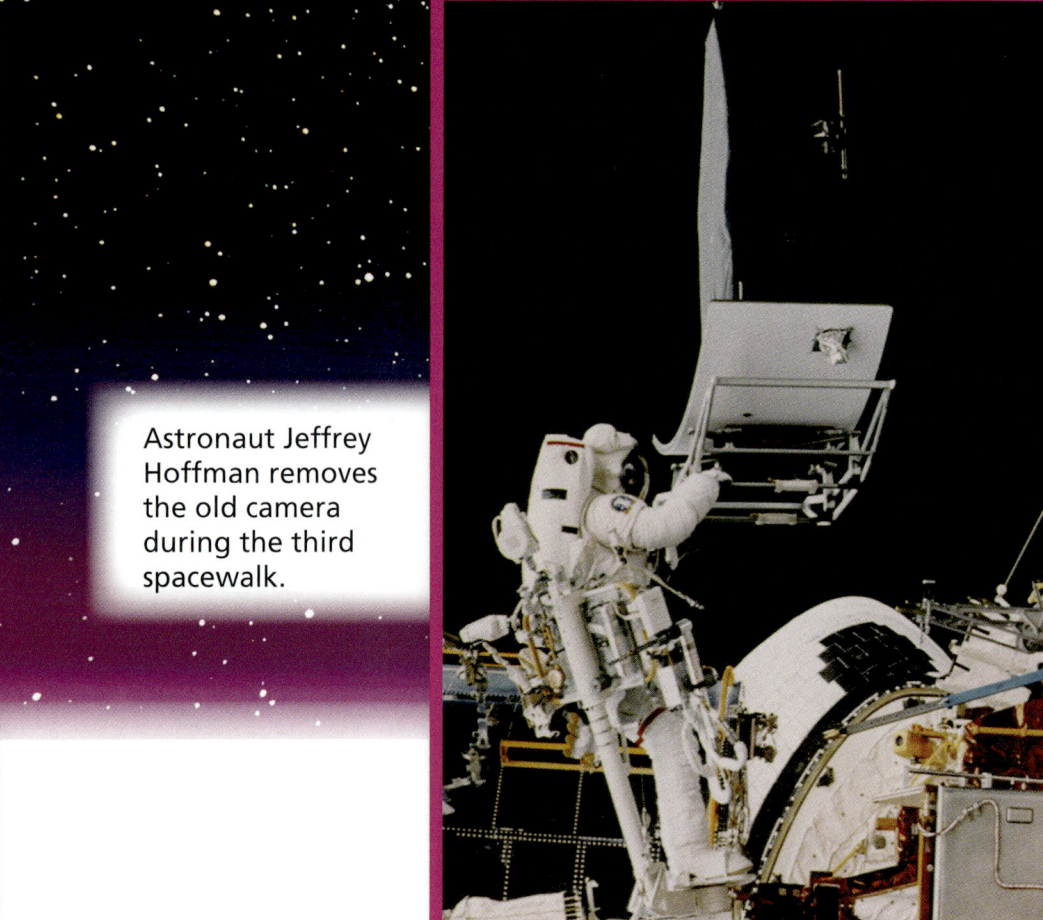

Astronaut Jeffrey Hoffman removes the old camera during the third spacewalk.

During the third spacewalk, Story Musgrave and Jeffrey Hoffman replaced a camera on Hubble. The new camera was very sensitive and could be easily damaged. The two astronauts had to work very carefully.

For this job, Jeffrey Hoffman stood at the end of the robotic arm. He held the camera while Story Musgrave took off the cover from its mirror. Then the two astronauts moved carefully to guide the camera in place in the telescope.

This photo shows Kathryn Thornton lifting the instrument that contains the mirrors to correct Hubble's vision before its installation.

On the fourth spacewalk, Kathryn Thornton and Thomas Akers installed the mirrors to correct Hubble's vision. It took almost seven hours to complete the job. The mirrors were in a metal box the size of a refrigerator. In space, it was weightless but still very hard to handle.

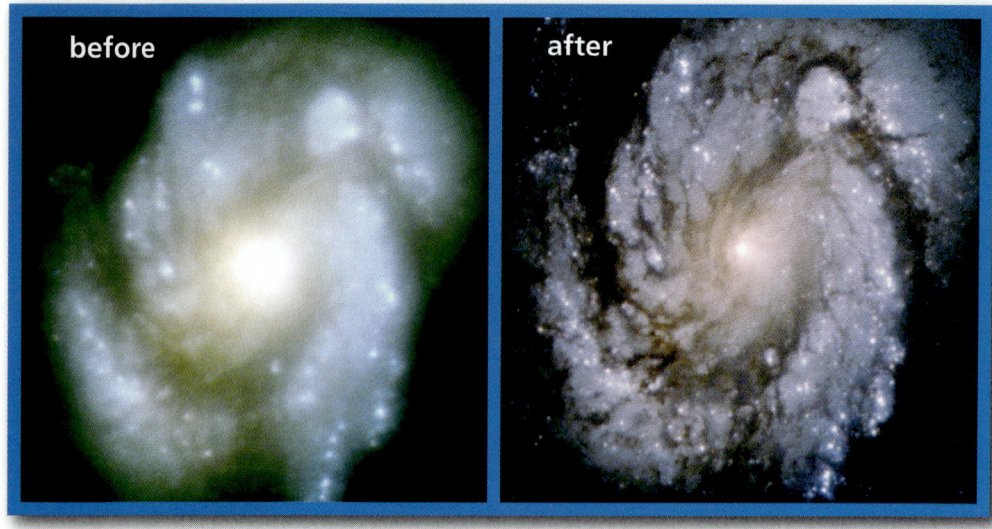

The before photograph shows Hubble's "vision" before it was corrected. The after photograph shows an image from the telescope after the first mission.

On the final spacewalk, Story Musgrave and Jeffrey Hoffman made sure that everything was closed up properly on the telescope. They also did some last repairs.

The astronauts finished their work and released Hubble back into orbit the next day. Then, after ten days of hard work in space, they went back home.

Back on Earth, the astronauts of *Endeavour* did not know right away if they had fixed Hubble. But a few days later, scientists tested Hubble. The images sent by Hubble were clear. The astronauts had done a very good job. Finally, Hubble worked beautifully!